November Rising
A Year Later

By
Claudia Patchen

Photographs by
Jennifer Patchen and
Claudia Patchen

KEY PEN PRESS

P.O. Box 167
Vaughn, WA 98394

November Rising
A Year Later

For more information please contact:

KEY PEN PRESS

P.O. Box 167
Vaughn, WA 98394

ISBN: 978-0692248478
Library of Congress Control Number: 2015941457

Patchen, Claudia, 1950-

November Rising: A Year Later

Search keywords: Suicide, mental illness, survivor, recovery, healing.

Printed in the United States of America

Table of Contents

For Jenny, Jen and Jennifer

Foreword

November Rising: A Poetic Journey was published a year before the present volume as a mother's exploration into her own journey through the suicide of her adult daughter, grief, and recovery.

When the book was released she had no idea how profoundly it might impact others. As a result of reading her work publicly and sharing her story she came to realize its power to touch so many others, most of whom had not even had a close family member die in such a tragic way. But really, the story is one of love and loss–the stuff of being human that we all share.

The present volume retains the most poignant pieces from the original book, but attempts to weave in new wisdom that can only come from experience–the experience of telling the story, touching others, and being touched in return.

–The Publisher

Acknowledgements

All I ever wanted was for my family to be alright–to love one another and show it in the happy places and hard spaces ... Would I do things different if allowed to live through it all again??? You bet! But that's hindsight with the 20/20 vision of things gone wrong. I feel as though I have come full circle in my life thus far and have "arrived at the beginning" to quote T.S. Elliot.

I have learned that blood *is* thicker than wine and it's my family I would thank above all else for, yes–giving me life and more importantly breathing love and memories and strengths and weaknesses into it. Thank you mom and dad–I love you!

Everyone I have known has been my teacher. I can honestly say I truly value what you taught me and I think of each of you fondly. Really!!! My husband, my sister (who lost her own little girl and without whom I wouldn't have made it through), my friend, Jackie, Lorraine Hart, whose November poem-a-day blog spurred me on, Danna Webster, Watermark Writers, and so many others. Yes, and my God–I love You and adore You. Thank You for not giving up on me.

–Claudia

We're All on a Journey

We're all on a journey
writin' our stories
fightin' for our lives
Will we make it? Authentic selves, intact???

Will we peer into that
clear pool and see the
reflection—that is us?
Complete, whole—good enough???

We're all on a journey
writin' our stories
will we make it—
                    to the Paradise—that is us?

The Children of the Courtyard

I awaken to the throbbing pain of what feels like illness—my head aches, my face feels flushed and hot and my eyes burn and sting. I see light outside, forcing its way through a 15 inch square, mold-speckled skylight/ventilator window of a 26 ft. trailer, covered by a cheap blue plastic tarp to keep the Northwest rains out. I imagine blue skies, but I know better.

I force myself out of bed extravagantly thinking, perhaps hoping, "am I dying???" I turn on the bright light over the pint-sized washbasin, mildly discolored with age and peer into the eyes starring back at me ten-times magnified. Gone are the clear eyes of youth. In their place are eyes, moss green, reticulated with a chestnut crown, variegated with intricate black hairpin stripes. They're not ugly eyes—they're eyes that have seen a lot--too much. I imagine that what appears as scar-tissued, off-white, is tinged with yellow from probably three years of more wine than I needed and too many, over-the-counter pills to ease the pain and hasten sleep. The tiny red blood vessels—oh, they come from pressure, no doubt about that—elevated blood pressure.

The eyes, the window to the soul, they say. My friend, Jo says that you can see the devils in one's soul through the unclear, yellowed whites of the eyes. I suspect that's liver disease. Call it myth, call it social construct, or call it reality, I'm wary, just the same.

My friend Paul is a self-confessed eccentric. His best friend chides him, that he's not

2

normal—one plumb off center. I chuckle and believe him. On Sunday mornings, I sit on the front row of our tiny community and watch him lovingly prepare and elevate the host of Life— the wafer—the Body of Christ. As he lifts his eyes toward heaven, where we hope all is fresh and clean—his grey/blue hazel eyes never fail to amaze me with their crystal clear, snow-white, clarity, pureness and beauty—the eyes—the window to the soul—the barometer of internal health.

Still, I force myself out of bed, for I have a story to write—a story of life and death—a story of blindness and vision—a story of question and hope. I have entitled it, "The Children of the Courtyard." The names have been changed to protect the wounded, the innocent, the forgiven, and the guilty. Who are, "The Children of the Courtyard," you might ask? I would say, they are us and they are legion and they are fine. They are pitiable, they are brave beyond measure and sometimes they are loathsome. Sometimes they are sad, fragile and lonely and sometimes they are lifted up toward heaven as embued with light in a chorus of angels. Always, they are "real," loaned for a season—"ours" and "not-ours."

As you read this—think of Sophocles' Oedipus Rex—the prophecy, the tragedy, the hope, and the journey—"I was blind, but now I see."

At the time of writing this story, it's been three long years since our daughter's violent, tragic, self-imposed death. I have pondered everything relentlessly. My son Joel says often, "Mom, stop thinking so much—you'll drive yourself crazy," but I can't help myself. I'm obsessed with it all—with memory--as if to let go of it, would be to lose her forever. So, I think and write and wonder, "what was it all about? What does it mean? How might it have been different? What makes a twenty-eight-year-old do such a thing?" The answers elude me but the process helps.

Like Oedipus of old, the story begins with a prophecy, spoken over her at the tender age of eight. Following moderate failure in business, our young family sought refuge in the military, in the midwest "Bible-Belt." While there, we corporately found "Religion," were baptized in the Rubideau River and then were ushered off to the Christian Mecca of Tulsa, OK where my husband would serve and teach in a well-known Christian University.

Miraculously, it seemed that doors were closed and doors were opened as to where we should live, where the children should go to school and especially where we should attend church. We fell right into a newly established storefront "Rainbow" church, as it was being called because of all the different ethnic groups that attended. The group was excited, alive and ready to change the world. Sunday nights were "family night." The now famous pastor always had something intimate and really special planned—visiting ministers or just his heart-to-heart chats of what life in the ministry was really about. These were special times. We were among the esteemed, first "pillar families" of the church—my husband being a University Professor at the pastor's alma mater and all. Our daughter had befriended a young singing star of the church and the two of them would sit on the front row.

This particular Sunday night, a prophetess was coming to town. This was always high drama, as they came with great power and flair and dynamism. Excitement charged through the air as people 'expected' to hear in a sense, a letter from home and for some 'lucky people,' usually the regular workers in the church, to be singled out of the crowd for more personalized words of encouragement or praise or whatever.

Well, this lady was different than most. She seemed a humble, unassuming lady from South Texas where she spent many years working as a maid for Kenneth Copeland's household. She was not glitzy, but pleasant and soft-spoken though her words were markedly tinged with authority. I like what she had to say about things—it centered with my soul. Even then, I was somewhat cynical and rarely went along with the crowd.

She gave a few general prophecies and then the room suddenly quieted to a hush and then she started to cry. She kept her head down as if she were seeing or hearing something and continued to sob and cry. About this time, my husband leaned over to me and whispered in an insistent tone, "she's going to call Jennifer," and that's exactly what she did. The prophetess looked up, motioned to our Jennifer who was seated on the front row and said, "Come here, Sweetie." Jennifer, being shy by nature, got up and quickly searched the crowd, shot me a look of puzzlement and went up. She looked so tiny and forlorn, lost in her big furry winter coat. The lady put her arms around Jennifer, enveloped her and now was just sobbing without restraint. She told Jen that Jesus wanted her to know that He just loved her so much and she was to never forget that. She seemed to search for words, then said that she saw people making fun of her, but that she was loved and that God was going to use her in His kingdom and then it was done. The rest I didn't or couldn't hear or that was all.

It was unusual yes—but for some strange reason, we did not pay much attention until some ten years later when her life took a very dark turn. She would have mood swings of extreme highs and extreme lows—probably we thought the result of teen-age hormones and moving a lot. The truth was, this was the beginning of a ten-year bout with hell on earth, especially for her and for all who loved her, as well.

Slipping back to the night of her death...as fate would have it, I was just finishing up my final paper for a class in Abnormal Psychology, where I had frantically been looking for all the answers. I tacked on this ending as I sought to hold on to my sanity.

It reads:

I hope you don't mind but I would like to close with a postscript to the abnormal psych paper I was writing the night our daughter took her life. It highlights and encapsulates the needs and purposes of my three favorite modes at the time. And now I'd say existential has superseded them all. Thank you in advance for sharing in my pain.

Postscript: I know this is an unusual paper but I am allowing myself this liberty. If I don't, this personality might just fragment and scatter onto that sea of blissful forgetfulness, where fantasy presides over reality and pain can no longer be felt—because—last night, we found out that our daughter had taken her own life. Life on this earth must have become more than she could bear. As I sat outside her tiny cottage watching the police, examiners, and assorted workers doing what they do, I thought of Freud and Jung and Cognitive Theory. And in between my my sobs, my quiet screams and my prayers, I thought, "You know, Freud was right, we're all hopelessly flawed in one way or another." Then I thought, "Jung was right, we are more than a body and a mind—we are a soul." And then I thought, "The cognitive therapists are right in that, if you can change your thinking, you can change your life, but who can give you a heart to change your mind and treat your body right?" With our smattering of knowledge, we do our best. The fire chaplain helped me more than anyone else in those cold dark hours of night. He was human. He told me all the things he thought of with his heart, during times like these. We talked of God, cremation, personal choices, and broken marriages—his and mine. He prayed for me, and the landlord who I'd come to know, allowed me to cry and grip him with anguished hands.

Two weeks earlier, a little ten year-old resident of the courtyard cottages had built a small shrine in the truncated lap of a massive oak tree outside Jen's door. She had placed a small kneeling angel with a sign, scribbled in a child's hand, "This is the guardian angel sent to watch over the courtyard." This is where we will hold our small service to say our final good-bye to our dearly beloved Jennifer with the good heart—Mom loves you! It is finished—there is nothing more to say. See you later—we'll laugh—we'll talk—we'll hug.

***

But of course, there is always more to say—especially when writing is what you do. The writings in this small book are my words to say...from that November night when our Jennifer arose to ten years later when I symbolically arose and that is why I have entitled it ... "November Rising."

Evening of ... "The Dream" ...

Evening of ... "the Dream" ...
Pulled the door shut
on the night seen
of cop cars encircling
the tiny cottage with room
enough only for me to slip
in.
What a bevy of activity recalled
as examiners did their job
a backlit scene but
less than thirty feet away--my baby girl
all grown-up and dead.
Back home again, I pull the shade
on day and slip into a sleepful
extended journey ...
I see her in a land of light
skipping gaily on an upwardly curving sidewalk
to what resembles a Mr. Roger's
neighborhood.
Her honey-red hair is flowing thick about
her shoulders--with
a dancer's lilt, she turns to me

smiles broadly and beams to my brain

"I'm fine--in the same neighborhood—

just a little farther out" and gives me

that sweet wry grin.

"I want to go with you," I say with

all that is in my heart.

She gently nods, "No," bends over and

reaches down to the sidewalk

and tosses me a light lavender

velour soft sweater and says,

"Here--this will keep you warm--

wear it to cover your heart--

then, off she "is," happily

disappearing--off into a

Sunrise skyline ... out of sight

        but, never out of reach ...

If People Want to Know Me

She emerged from her room

Late in life

Gone were the accouterments of

Her former life

*The seven rings from her ear And assorted
piercings–Her face unadorned now and*

Plain for all to see

*A moment's respite from a psychotic
haze"Jen," I said, "Something's Different–
what did you do?""Oh," she said, with the
calmestDemeanor, "I took them all out.*

*From now on...if people want to'Know me'–
they'll have to 'Talk to me.'*

I understood.

She had had a 'change of heart.'

Anorexia Nervosa

How very fitting, that Susan Bordo should use the revealing copy from a Crystal Lite television commercial to poetically depict the delicate but sturdy line between body, politics, power, and culture: "I believe in being the best I can be, I believe in watching every calorie..." the ad says. How deceptively cool, calculated and in total control that sounds. How very untrue! She explores these complex phenomena with crystal-clear insight and careful explanation, causing us to question a culture that feeds its own, such disease producing concepts. She uses the axes of dualism, control, and gender/power to explain and show where and how anorexia fits into the larger scheme of what we call culture. I especially appreciated her acknowledging the multidimensional aspects of the disorder, with its familial, perceptual, cognitive, and possibly even biological aspects contributing to the "final common pathway," along the continuity axes.

It is important to note that this psychopathology is not new, dating back to the times of St. Augustine, Plato, and Descartes; hence its dualistic nature. Always, in these cases the mind is separate from the body or the spirit. The body is seen or felt as alien or 'not-me,' as well as a sort of prison, swamp, cage, or other limiting or confining place. The 'body-as-the-enemy,' is another common aspect, always at war with the spirit, requiring self-control, until control eventually becomes the central issue. It's clear to see that there can be no, 'peace-of-mind,' to speak of, when the body is at war with the mind or spirit, until it is without desire, hunger, need, or existence. They seem indeed, a prisoner in their own bodies.

One could well understand that with these distressing images, continual struggles, and battles waging within, one could quite naturally feel out of control. It's been stated that their perfectionistic tendencies exacerbate the problems, as well. The typical themes of their existence resonate with emphasis on will, purity, and perfection. They become tyrants or dictators over their own bodies, perceiving themselves without control over anything else in their lives. I think this is an area where men too, get lured into the illusion of control and self-mastery, in our out-of-control culture, with its emphasis on achievement and obsessive success. One wonders if this perfectionistic, youth-oriented culture, truly believes we don't HAVE to die–or worse yet–grow old. Powerlessness is the sad hallmark of this affliction.

That brings us to the gender/power axis, since ninety percent of all anorectics are women, the statistics hint that this plight is not gender-innocent. The distorted body image reminds us that the woman's body is indeed a political space and in our fitness-crazed culture, we are often made to feel that we take up too much space. Not only that, but because the typical traditional American male is uncomfortable with the archetypal female aspects of his own self, he's equally uncomfortable with our blatantly female aspects, as well. Young females caught in the crossfire of these adult male/female conflicts often wear the scars. They don't know whether to reject the traditional female roles or to remain preadolescent in their bodies, by voluntary starvation, or both. When Bordo brought up the fact that often we, as women are made to feel that we eat too much, need too much, want too much, express too much, cry too much, etc., and that there is an idealized female image of a, "ministering angel-type; sweet, gentle, domestic, without intensity or personal ambition," of any sort, I thought of Scarlett O'Hara from "Gone with the Wind." Remember sweet Melanie–mealy-mouthed, fragile, pale, and insipidly-kind, Melanie? I can hear Scarlett saying, " Oh fiddley-dee!" as she attends to Melanie's every little need, right to the end. Scarlett was brazen, tough and strong–and yes, conniving and needy. (And my point is???) Perhaps, the gender/power issue is one of long-standing–that NEEDS to be addressed, regularly. There does seem to be a cyclic nature to the conflict–times of historic change–new possibilities and old expectations. We need to make peace with

14

it and each other, for our childrens' sake–for our cultures' sake–for 'we' are society.

So, what do we see? We see that it might appear that the American anorectic could indeed bear the "unbearable weight," of our culture's ills.

I know I have seen it played out before my very own eyes. I did not recognize the symptoms in my young husband, but helplessly, I watched them emaciate my daughter. It was co-morbid with other ailments, but all the aforementioned mind-sets and symptoms were present. It's true. Hindsight is 20/20. It's so much clearer now. It's not about blame–it's about cause and effect. We need to understand the correlations. When I met my husband (my ex-), he used to run 20 miles, 3 times per week, sometimes with diagnosed stress fractures in his feet. When Jen was 18, I heard her tell our sons, "Don't eat candy, you might get fat and then Dad won't love you anymore." In her later stages, once psychosis had set in, she'd talk about aliens and clones and how she could see her body organs on the floor, in front of her. After she died, I found stacks of index cards with careful, hand-written recipes–food she wouldn't allow herself to eat. She was obsessed with food.

So, what do we see? We see a crystallization of culture–a crystal-clear image of a feminine mystique, demystified, de-valued, distorted and destroyed, by time-honored fallacies and misdirected values–perhaps, perpetuated by the likes of you and me. We see nations in need of drastic change.

"Little Faces"

Dreamed a dream last night...
a mailman with a message
and a man with a surprise for me
cloaked in a beaming smile.
"I have something for you,"
he said and climbed what
looked like a wooden kiva ladder
in what felt like an Eastern
marketplace.
He reached far inside the upstairs
storage space and pulled out
a HUGE red paper lantern with
pure gold-edged lining...
wasn't sure of the meaning of
it all but it "felt" good.
In the imagination of my
eye, I participated in the
ancient Buddhist lantern festival
honoring those who have passed.
I saw the lovely "little faces" in my
heart--many faces I knew--many
faces, I didn't, but I did. I saw little

Gramma, Aunt Lily, my dad, but

the most precious of all, were

little 7 year old Julie and my very

own Jen--all beaming brightly in

the lovely lit sky.

A wondrous event--even in a dream--especially, in a dream.

Does that make me an honorary

Buddhist? ;)

The Dreamer...

Orbits ...

She orbits our earth

we orbit one-another

calamity strikes--obliteration

affects us all

we, the mobile of her life

she, the pebble in our pond

the sun in our heaven

felt by all~forever.

Surviving ...

In my rude awakening
I lost my compass
The earth turned to sand
And the sky became hollow,
Colorless & non-existent.
A shade was pulled upon
The Window of my Life.
I was as one in, "The
Night of the Living Dead."
I slept the sleep of a drugged
Victim.
All nerve-endings pulled
Away from the wound.
I sought solace in solitude-
Or mindless activity.
I stared a lot—I slept a lot.
I prayed.
My prayers were like one—
Scratching.....
On the interior surface of
A blackboard coffin.

Pleas — scribbled in the scrawl,

Of a mad-woman

Mad with grief — insane with pain.

There is no Common Prayer

For the newly bereft.

There are no words of comfort —

No pill, no treatment — to ease the throbbing pain.

Only time & space & sunshine

Can begin to soothe the cavity — we call

Sudden tragic loss.

The Paradox of "Being" ...

Somewhere between the Death
        of my firstborn
And the Birth of my first–Grandchild
I found my Life.

I found it teetering
        As on the edge of a cliff
Not sure as to whether, it would fall
Crash & become the ruins on the
Canyon floor below
                or
Take wings & fly–like a Phoenix
Escaping, the charred ruins of recent events.

                I was uncertain.
                I was unmovable.
                I was unafraid.

"No longer did I expect great things.
No longer did I dread bad things.
Where I dwelt was not a bad place.
It was just, a place."

I was luckier than some.

I was unluckier than others.

I was neither happy, nor sad.

"I was content–content to live "my" Life
Whatever that life might be.
I'd play the cards that I was dealt
Trusting, the dealer in the sky."
Poised, I sat fanning my face with

My dealt hand...

I was strong, fearless & wild.

I was surrendered, utterly

dependent & free.

I was a child–a child of the

King.

I was a chicken, scratching for seed in the dirt.

I was a player, in a three-ring circus.

I was a laid-back rocker, in a rock-n-roll band.

I was a Lover of people & Life.

I, WAS the Prince & the Pauper. I WAS the Princess
& the Pea.

I slid down mushroom stalks, to worlds I've yet to see.

I stand on my head, to see the Truth.

I paint my scrunched-up face, with squinty-eyed lids.

I bark at the dogs that sniff at my feet.

I caress, the toad at my head.

I have been stripped, of my support, my defenses

                  and

My veneers.

                Who am I?

I was–now, I am–and I'm yet to be–

                The child–the child–the child–

                of a king.

Candles ...

Give me a tree to hug
and I'm grounded to the earth.
Give me a candle to
burn & I'm melting
into eternity.
Give me a bundle of
meaningful candles burning
together & I'm a fricken'
funeral pyre dissolving
into ether nothingness &
enjoying the trip--
Holy campfire encircling Life ...

The Parable of the Antherium Family

or

How to Stand on Your Own Two Feet, Together

or

Co-Dependent No More

There one was a wife who worshiped her husband. It was her desire to please him in every way. But, of course this was not possible. In her attempt however, she nearly gave up her soul and at the same time created a monster of a relationship between herself and her husband. She followed him around like a puppy dog and he avoided her at every turn–feeling awful about it, but not knowing that her idol-worship was suffocating him.

The teen-age daughter, being perceptive by nature, recognized the dis-ease and thrashed about with all her might, in an effort to break free. Because you see, she loved them both very much. Her thrashing and kicking and running led her into one precarious situation after another, until at last she found herself-- a drug addict. The parents sought help and God intervened. That's what this story is all about.

It's Mother's Day, 1994. Mom and Dad and the two teen-age boys have moved to Hawaii eight months prior–minus the twenty-one-year-old daughter, who has chosen to stay behind, quit college, and live together with her boyfriend. The situation troubles the parents, but with much on their hands and seeing very little recourse, they give them their love and move on. Five months later, the boyfriend is senselessly, tragically murdered while delivering pizza in what would become a landmark case in California's history, but that means little to the daughter, who lost her "love."

Meanwhile, back at Mother's Day, in the midst of trials (literally), ill health, and counseling, Mother's Day arrives, and the boys, in an attempt at normalcy and happiness, buy Mom an Antherium plant–an exotic plant of ruby-red, waxen-like beauty. Good-naturedly, they tease her that she is NOT to kill it–as is her custom. So, with trepidation, she tends the beloved plant. Throughout the next three years of trial and instability for the daughter and family, the plant continues to live and squeak out the perennial single bloom.

Then, the fourth year, all "hell" appears to break loose. Just as life for the family was beginning to return to normal, the revelation came from 2000 miles away, that the daughter was on heroin and to make matters worse–was on the run.

At last, they were forced to seek help. During these sessions, the wife felt that she began to see a "picture" of what was going on. Strange as it sounds, her attention was mysteriously drawn to the Antherium Plant. She noticed that there were actually two clumps at the base of the plant, but only one bloom had been coming. And to make matters worse, the plant looked root-bound and was growing weak.

The plant began to obsess her. I'm sure those around her were concerned, but they were patient and kind, "She's under duress," they probably thought. She discussed the plant at counseling sessions and as the urgency to separate the two clumps grew to an alarming pitch, (reading much into it), the people began to fear that a divorce was on the horizon. But all that she saw was a plant and what had to be done to save it. For weeks she knew she had to separate them and transplant them, but she didn't have the soil or the pots, the emotional energy, or the time. She fretted.

Finally, as the family counseling reached a fevered pitch and she could take it no more, she ran out back to separate the clumps before the whole plant died and all was lost.

She transplanted with reckless abandon, using whatever soil was around, readying the two clay pots intended and carefully separating the two clumps, which came apart with ease. But then, to her horror, having come this far, she realized, the clay pots were too small–much too small and their roots lay exposed–what was she to do?!

Frantically, she looked around the small yard. There, in the corner was a huge sunflower seed bucket, already half-filled with soil. That's what she'd do. She'd just plant the clumps further apart, with plenty of space to grow and put lots of soil around the roots. They'd probably grow together again, but only to be put in a larger pot again. Yes–what relief–what joy, and then laughter at the amazing outcome. They didn't need to be in separate pots after all–only space to be, two strong individual plants, coming together to form a more perfect union. Whew! What a novel thought.

And–the fate of the Antherium plant? I kid you not–very shortly thereafter, a bloom grew on the one clump, new leaves emerged and low and behold, blooms that customarily take months to come and weeks to open up, just magically emerged. Two additional blooms emerged on one and the biggest thrill of all, was that just as the daughter called, and went into detox and treatment, a HUGE bloom came forth on the other clump. Amazingly, now there were five blooms in all–one for every member of the family. So, just before leaving Hawaii, what we'll call, "The Antherium Family," was restored and bloomed and flourished in the, "Sonflower," seed container. The Antherium family rejoiced at the amazing coincidence– coincidence–I think not! And who knows, perhaps they lived happily ever after. Oh no, that would be a fairytale and this is a parable and a parable is a story about truth.

Riding the Crest of a Wave

It was 1987, or there-abouts, were we riding the crest of a wave?! Something 'broke' inside of me…I started writing poems, I had a big dream.

It was a spiritual divorce, of sorts…something to be reckoned with…over time.

It was like the continental divide of two souls…nothing left but to wash downhill, to separate seas…finding our own little tributaries…bleeding, instead of singing as we bubbled over the stones of life.

I was told, 'it was not—my problem,' but I couldn't fathom, the wake. I retreated into fantasy, pretended to be numb…I felt betrayed, bewildered, beyond hope.

Then came, the emotion of snow or should I say, the lack of emotion…it freezes, it covers, whatever is there, for a season…'til later.

I Remember

I remember, a young lad of nineteen
taking his anger, hurt, and frustrations
off to a war--that couldn't be won.

I remember being fifteen, and
unable to carry that emotional weight.
I remember, writing a letter.

I remember you
coming back nine months
later--changed.

Your blond hair--tinted shades of red
from the earth you crawled.
Your skin-- burned by the sun.

I remember the stories--you didn't tell
of pulling your buddies out
in various stages of death.

I remember the nightmares
and tears
you tried to hide.

I remember the sacrifice you made
and what it cost you
and our family.

I remember--
that our boys did not
have to go....

        and, I am grateful.

Indigo Jeans ...

Memories of indigo jeans

               and

tiny little ski-slope butts.

Those jeans were so soft

                        washed a million times,

they were

               and

faded out to that light blue hue

                        shared with the sky over

Malibu

Pepperoni pizza with grease

                        dripping down our arms

to elbows

milk—milk—must have more milk!

We were so creative then

                        fashioning sand candles

in our afternoon delight

messy—in our tiniest of cottages but

               no worries...

We were young—we were free

               and

far, far from home...

Our Life's work was

                          to Learn & Love &
Play!

We were so much wiser then

                          I'm younger than that
now.

Shape-shifter ...

*A lover, a friend & a former spouse once said to me,
"A rose is a rose is a rose," and I thought with bitter
rancor, oh yeah sure & a bitch is a bitch is a bitch.*

*Then time went by and I thought, well maybe he
might say, "I'm so glad that thorns have roses."*

*And now — as time goes by and I gaze at those three
blood-red roses, cradled in the rough hands of life-
long devotion, I think, "A three-part chord is not
easily broken" — love endures — just changes its shape
and sometimes, location.*

Jesus, Jazzman & White Zin …

Jesus, Jazzman & White Zin … We share the share the same white vein. We tumble thru alleyways…we bounce off castle walls! We laugh, we cry, we wail, for no good reason… We fill up & we spill out unto humanity because, we can…because, we care… because, we must-- because, we must care… or we wouldn't do it. Jesus, Jazzman & White Z—I love you!

At the Corner of East & West

At the corner of East & West

their love lay down together.

He slathered her with butterfly kisses.

She responded with lavish joy.

They consummated their commitment

in the field of hopeful bliss.

Without a word, heav'n was forever changed.

The two cemented time & place together.

The skies opened-up & received them —

forgotten — never!

For now, there was room for everyone

space to breathe, to move about, to know, to love,
forever-more!

Rejoice with us, as we treasure the love

                              found on the corner of
East & West.

I Am Camera—Hear Me ROAR

"I am camera—

hear me ROAR,"

said the sweet young thing

inside

taking shots, we'd best

ignore

to grace our inner pride.

I can still see the

chawed-on ribs, up-close

on someone's dainty plate

nasty bones exposed, red

blood deposed--a vision--

I still hate.

Aversion therapy, I called it then

a vegan--called it truth.

Lovingly, I finger each photo now

exposing our uncouth.

Flaxen Seed Hair & Button Brown Eyes

Flaxen seed hair & button brown eyes

a study in pink, surrounded

must've felt good, swaddled in

warmth, for the ferry journey--over

one mass to another, divided by water

the wind, whipping sounds though our hairs

jolly & carefree—happy, we were—

a moment in time—suspended

time holds no bounds—

I'm there with you now—

the three of us—mommy, daddy &
jenny—united!

Dreamy Visions of Johnny Depp, I See

Dreamy visions of Johnny Depp, I see
Layed-out in his opiate den.
Golden coins put his eyes to rest.
How will he ferry cross the 'Mercy?'
Is there a river named, 'Mercy?'
Or a 'Sea of Glass' to the other side?
Who will provide the 'coins' of passage???
I suspect, it's already been done…

The price has been paid, for all…
It's a peaceful passage—I suspect.

Perhaps…

Gandhi is the ferryman
happy Buddha, waves farewell, from the shore
Jesus, has paid the price
                              &
Allah, overarches all…
against a backdrop of MLK's
soulful refrain…
                         We 'have' overcome!'
Perhaps, perhaps, perhaps…
                         or, not.

Jenny Dear Poem ...

It was late summer 2001.

It was like a homecoming of sorts—family members called in on the winds from all points North, South, East and West. Our little Jenny dear--come home to heal, to hope, to speak her mind??? We'll never know. But all converged on the North West to be with one another, one last season.

We had moved her out of our small rental into a Courtyard Cottage nestled among several others in hopes that the incremental independence would spur her on to stronger emotional health. It didn't work. Her dad had already moved out several months prior, in hopes that the friction removed would foster healing in the females left behind—mom and daughter. She and her dad were estranged. It worked for a while. The boys and their partners now lived in neighboring communities.

The home-coming held the potential for happy endings. Trial and error—it was all trial and error.

We all enjoyed Friday night pizza get-togethers—so good to be all together after so many heartaches and so many years. She showed up more and more infrequently and stayed for shorter spells, when she did come. I soon became her only contact. We would meet at a favorite Chinese place about once a month— always, I would call and make the arrangements and like a gentle ghost she would float through the visits, with downcast eyes.

Nine-eleven had just happened. After all the father/daughter drama, her dad and I had just agreed to an amicable divorce after thirty-four years of marriage. So much fragile stuff to discuss, I thought.

She called me—the first time in a long while. Let's meet for lunch, Mom. Ok, I say. I am encouraged beyond words. She has bright strong energy behind her voice.

I pick her up--we order our usual favorites. She eats voraciously, which delights my mama nature.

Guess what? I say. Soon I'll be done with school and finally get my certificate.

Oh good, she says brightly. I hope to be gone by the time that happens.

You do, I reply. Where are you going?

Oh, I don't know, she says, I was thinking maybe Vancouver, B.C. or something.

The rest of the visit was upbeat and pleasant. I drive her home. I give her a quick kiss on the cheek.

I love you Jen, I say to her. She rolls her eyes at me with a gentle smile, I know you do Mom. And with that, she's out the door....

for the last time.

It's a Dangerous Game

It's a dangerous game—prophecy is

Even if you're for real—you'd better run for cover

Go hide in the hills—better yet—a cave!

If you're not—for real

You've got hell to pay

If you still believe in it—that is.

Gone are the days, of tight-knit groups

Who grieve blood & tear

For a brother or sister-dear—in question.

Repent & mend your ways—they'd say. We'll help.

Or, the board will meet & discuss your claims.

Or, stone him & off with his head. That's when he runs!

It's not that easy, when you're gone astray

Body, mind, soul & spirit will play you—all day

And through the night, as well.

Be not deceived—this is no small thing.

He who plays the prophet—will live to tell.

And the purveyor of justice? Fragrance or smell?

We all play our roles—cat, mouse, king & enabler
To name a few. But God rules the roost—we'll all
Get our due.

Where's God in all this? In this horrible plight?
Testing & weighing—listening & waiting, to see
what we'll ask?

I for one am glad that we—not any of us—is God!

A Century-old Hand-hewn Vessel

A century-old hand-hewn vessel

                    wobbles on the wind-rift sea

seventies' torched hard-wood style

                    once, a homey-abode

now haunted by charred remains.

A shadowy couple wander the top deck.

The children below cower in corners

for dear life.

There are no corners in a century-old galleon.

A wayward wind topples the bon-fired abode.

The craft top-sides and turns

asunder.

A mother's tortured wail carries on the wind, "What

will become of the kids?"

A burial at sea—a funeral pyre.

New life begins…

                on, another plane.

Barn Stormin' ...

Musing thru 34 years of life-imbued stuff thrown in the barn by a frantic runaway.... Too many years later—it's time to "face the music"—turn back toward the past and peel the layers apart—keep what's usable, of value and treasured and throw away the rest...a "work" begun in poetry, years and years before.

Most everything smells of mold and must—of course, this is Washington. Zillions of mice have made their homes with the fabric of our lives—perfect—seems only fair—one man's lost treasure—another's trappings of survival—but ohhh—the stench! (note to self—never use staples or paper clips on sacred papers—they rust and bleed during long times of exile and asylum.

Pretty much glided thru the bulk of it, but got whip-lashed, blind-sided, bushwhacked by the fresh-faced family portraits—all five of us—younger than Life—layered in shades of sky-blue. What to do with the perfect view of blue—got lost inside the beautiful clear-skinned smiles and then I notice something...the beautiful ornate frame is perfect, except for one small detail: about every 14 inches all around the frame are what look like spider-web nests where very ornate filigree used to be. It's grotesque—in a poetic sort of way. My heart engages in despair and screams out..."That, is what you call divorce! That is what you call divorce!" Something once so

50

fine, spidered with the webs of tragedy and divorce. "What do I do with it?! What do I do with it? I let it go—it's time to let it go. "Plenty of good memories to hold onto—I take the meat and leave the bones— BURY the bones, in fact—in ritual affair—DUMP RUN!

Barn Stormin'Days—garbage, Goodwill and useful and valued treasures. The barn is now a cavern, of untold possibilities.

These Foundational Truths ...
We Hold to be True...

These foundational truths... we hold to be true...

Love never dies, the spirit has wings and roots connect us to this earth...for a season...

Me, myself & I

Faithful

There she is,
faithful as the moon,
the night.

Lost to the Dawn ...

Lost to the Dawn...the three wrestled the waters and the winds through the eve

only to lose the battle to the dawn.

The pink sky warning in the morning, arrived just a tad too late.

Run aground, come day, the vessel found its destiny as a sailors' coffin.

The Cross marks the spot.

Standing on the Precipice

Standing on the precipice of my Life...seeing at once,
beyond all that doesn't matter.

The Lure of Blue...

Layers of light, layers of depth, layers of color...I'm going in. Sucking air from a plastic tube, with one too many weights about my waist...I crawl and clutch at the sand beneath me--I'm going in. The tinny sound of silence surrounds me. Bubbles of air tickle my ears with a new sound of freedom. I want to be free. I fumble...release a weight or two. Perfect! Now, I'm a fish...one with the sea. A new-comer...yes, but free. I reach my arms in front of me and roll sideways, over and over—I'm an underwater astronaut—free from gravity—free to be me, or whatever I want. Curling up tight and rolling forward—I'm an underwater rolly polly bug—imagine that. Stretching out softly, arms and legs, closing my eyes and free-floating—suspended, deeply in blue—I'm a sting-ray. I'm one with the sea and I'm free—free from blue.

Are You Here, Are You There—Are You

I can't see you from here. Are you here, are you
there—are you

every-where???

Then again, maybe you're no-where –No! Never!

You're my very present help in time of need—
purrrrr!

That settles it—I think I'll take a nap…

These Hands ...

These hands love to whomp fannies in a playful way

all ages, all sizes —yes—I am a certified

                            'Fanny

Whomper'

ask those who know me well... whose fannies I've
been known

                      to whomp.

These hands have felt the subtle warmth of sexual
love, ignited

 setting my heart ablaze.

These hands, I mutilate down to the quik—when
stressed

my sign to me of needed—self-care.

These hands have tenderly felt, the 'tracks' of her
tears down

her arm, carefully covered by long sleeves.

These hands have 'felt' the hole in His hand, like
Thomas.

These hands—have felt, caressed and bled and
prayed...

Often.

Friday the 13th Prompt: The Return of Color…

You died suddenly, one late November day & a shade was pulled on my life. Everywhere I looked, I saw shades of gray & midnight black. I hid—I sought solace in God and solitary confinement with simple routines. I continued only a single daily activity outside my walls with people I barely knew. As I drove to & from each day, I marveled at the literal lack of color. I thought maybe I was mad—I didn't care. I surrendered to the all & nothing. Then one glorious spring morning, it happened—color—everywhere—color! I was still alive & you were still with me.

LOSS ...

We who allow loss

To define us

find a certain comfort

in wrapping that drab

dark blanket around us —

It's dependable — it's safe —

It's comforting — it's always there.

It serves us.

Without it — our heart

grows cold from the

fresh wind of change.

It's a decision we make

to stay the addiction

we've grown to love —

a certain sadness.

Sometimes, when we venture

out — we set ourselves up

for certain failure, by

choices made, on some level

60

that we know will let us down

so, we can wrap another dark blanket

of a similar shade around us--again.

Perhaps, we think our heart needs it

to feel—to create—to be—

                                    Us.

I wonder......

Dualities ...

Yesterday the storm—today the perfect calm

highest peaks to deepest holes

brand new life to ancient death

here today—gone tomorrow

light—dark

good—bad

wrong—right

shadow—light

feelin' good—feelin' bad

I'd like to scream.

*Me—I slip & slide—on the teeter-totter spectrum of
life*

living mostly in the shades of gray—occasionally

confronting my black & white issues...

The teeter-totter spectrum

prayin' for a small fulcrum & slidin' skill

to soften the bumps...

the 'perfect' symbol of balance

in the sand...the zebra...breakthrough...

a union of opposites!

Mirror Mirror ...

Mirror Mirror....

On the wall

Show me sweet pretties

Hear my low call.

Of a night-full of barking dogs and hyped-up drama — deluded fur.

Oblivion to most, but nerve-wracking to me: only "I," left to secure a solution to this monstrous invasion of "my" privacy.

It's 2:43 and the ranting continues — coddled and re-tucked in, works for five minutes — screaming "shut-up," works for three — slamming doors — satisfying, but doesn't change a thing.

I am alone in this — what shall it be???

Hark, my door has a lock — a symbol of safety — I lock my door and drug my brain with "A", and proceed to "la la land," where I dream of soundproofed backyard doggy castles where four-legged friends can play out their deluded game and leave us to our rest. We'll call it Canine Western State Mental Hospital — sweet sleep — at last...

The late quiet aftermath of morning, leaves me feeling groggy and unable to think through the pasty dawn of day. Nothing left to do but write…Maybe a rational solution can be found and the delusion will be gone at dawn, maybe some distant neighbor will shoot them, maybe I will move away and Mirror Mirror…you will see me rested, clear and Hopeful…maybe…Let's leave this tru-life nightmare behind and go get something to eat….to be continued…

Write is Might….

Had a Bad Day in My Body, Yesterday

Had a bad day in my body, yesterday. Last night, I slept until I felt better — no matter how long it took.

Don't much like to think of...'up the road' these days — just enjoying the here and now — as best I can.

Dreamt of eating fish, I did and preparing to perform a surgery I wasn't sure I was qualified to perform — so mostly just ate the fine fish they served me, in silence...

Felt so much better, after a super night's sleep — maybe further down the road or up the road, I'll sleep longer and be completely well and wake up to the dawn 'feelin' soooo goood — that might be nice. ;)

65

Hello ...

They're doing it
again
the same time last year
and the year before
and the year before that.

The dogs howl—all three
In unison
A plaintive chorus—downstairs
just beneath my desk.

They know.
What do they know?
Can they see, hear and feel
like I do
that the veil is thin and
that you have stepped within
    our presence...
        to say hello?

I Went Down with the Titanic

I went down with the Titanic
last night. It wasn't all bad.
I can breathe water....

Jen was there!

It was like the most natural
thing in the world—being underwater.

She had set-up housekeeping
in the shed outside our house.

I stepped inside.
All the walls were painted deep-sea-blue.
Her guitar stood by the door
next to her well-traveled back-pack.

The place was all popped-out on the inside
With all kinds of interesting nooks and crannies—
homey.

She was comfortably seated across
From a couple of friends, unlike her
bedeckled in nose rings, lip studs and
various jewels in various places.

They were conspirators — speaking
In hushed voices.

It was so nice to see her!

I heard one say to her, "Shall we use different
names?"

She moved her head from side to side
with an air of confident, mature understanding.
"Nah," she smiled, "she's my mom."

It warmed my heart!

I peeked into an exposed little shoebox
painted the same deep-sea-hue.
Inside was a treasure trove of tiny little
sacred objects — shells, rocks and amazingly
many little fire-lit pieces of oil-soaked cotton
filling the space with a holy glow — puja-like!

I was so happy!

I found myself thinking, Oh I hope no one will make her go away.

The dream ended with the puzzling words, "some good came of it."

Jen—

You had a fast car
split this town before us
                  alone
but never.
We never had a chance
to catch ya, here.
You flew in the arms of
                  an angel
to a land where we'll all
                  one day, park.
I wonder, are you rockin' with
the angels, or hangin' alone
                  where you are?
Old soul—your eyes
revealed a story, deep with pain
wry smile, a candid humor.
You were real, you were human
you were lonely, you were ours
and we hold you gingerly in our
                  hearts...
as our journeys encompass one-anothers'
                  for eternity.
Godspeed, my sweet
                  mom

70

Baby …

The hoary face of age
punctuated by button-
brown eyes,
the sniffing snort at
the bedroom door,
belying the night
watches — to see
that I'm still safely there
so many gone now.
the harmless lipoma lumps
that can be felt but not
seen
the silken ears that slip smoothly
between my hands
the feather-like moist nose-kisses
caressing my unsuspecting
shins & ankles
the love, the care, the affection…
so needed at a time like this.

Who says that diamonds are a girl's best friend?!

Where's that Crumpled List

Where's that crumpled list
I wrote so many years ago—
looking for the love I thought I needed?
The perfect Mate—the perfect Lover
the perfect Friend

                    for me...
all the wonderful qualities--
lhut would make me, happy?

Well, I can't find it anywhere, but
I remember the lesson...
Year after year, I'd stumble
upon that list and finger it lovingly—
then one day, it hit me...
"Fuck that shit," as someone dear to me
would put it--
"That person—with those qualities—that's who
I wanna be!"

Looking in the window, instead of out the window
I try to nurse, that new-found knowledge—now.

I Love Lines …

I Love

Lines …

Photographic lines…

that lead the eye

up

modernistic lines on

high-rise towers…

winding lines, of

babbling brooks tumbling

to the sea

deep-creased lines on

ancient faces

revealing sweetness and pain.

I love lines…

I love the line in the sand

beyond which I will not go

because it is my right to

know

me

the highway that snakes through the
mountain
passes with precision and flow.

I love crosses and squiggles and
lines that are curly and go round
and round and round.

I dare say, I've never met a line
I did not like
but, if I had to choose —
I'd choose the line that goes
home — wherever that might be.

I LIKE …

I like …

Creative, clean, comfy,

Cozy

Responsible, caring & safe.

I Like…

reliable, responsive, rewarding

ALIVE

spontaneous, tried, substantial

No waif.

Little Girl, Little Girl

Little girl, little girl
what have you learned
that Love's best tutor is life
that a castle can become
your tomb
with a moment's notice or less
that you are your own Mother
Father, Lover, Friend and
More?

Little girl, little girl
who have you become
lion, tiger, bear, or deer
Phoenix rising through
a tear on your way to the sun?
Little girl, little girl—go your way
speak no more-- hear
no say...
you are your very own dear heart
now come on—act that way!
And one more thing—
did I ever say, Thank You, little girl?

The Lioness

Don't know much about Totem-ry--don't take much
to re-li-gio-sity

but the animals speak, just the same.

Atop my totem--a golden wheel, with two deer facing

                    and

a black crow sitting upon right deer's head.

Also there--big brown bear like one who dream-
walked

the dry, river-bed of memories past.

No worries tho', a powerful boar hangs out between
the chapel

and the pump house where we wash our clothes

                    and

spotted once, black beaver with his big toothy-grin

ferocious only when cornered--to protect the young.

A silent tear is spilt, when spotting dead raccoon at

roads' edge--playmates we are, at times.

A dolphin and a swallow must have their place
among the

                    totem's tale ...

why, because they swim the sea and air--like I would,
If I

                    could.

The dolphin is as smart as smart can be. And the
swallow--well

they're my family, returning yearly--thrilling me
with their

high-flying feats--making babies outside my window.

Well, by now, my totem is near complete with only
one left

                 to follow.

She roams from top to bottom and back again--a
stealth-

like, protective presence--a little un-nerving yes, but
only

                 IF...

menaced—she is the lioness.

New Love. Life Goes On ...

The Rosy blush of new

                    Love

I've already seen

                    flush across your face.

It's easier to look into you

                    than into me.

You're pale now, with fear

                    fear of moving

                    forward

or, pulling back.

The distance is high.

The water, far below — threatens peril

The trestle of support

                    seems, thin & wobbly

The hour, tenuous

The moment, precarious

                    but, precious.

A featherweight, could tip-the-scale

                    "which way to

                    go???"

Which way to go...

Only time will tell...but will He? I don't know. We'll see.

Then again...If I was you...I wouldn't do it.

He did.

I'm so glad, he did.

Spirals ...

... Took me 30 years to get back to the college learnin' of my dreams

Only one in the family who gave a 'hoot' about such things.

'First' social service, mental health class attended opened with a sacred object exercise—a symbol of our journey and our purpose—assigned by a curious fella whose favorite song was, I'm Being Followed by a Moon Shadow"—a priest, of all things, in a secular community college.

Two symbols, I chose, explained, and placed on the sacred alter—a metal coil—a spiral—that fell out of the toilet paper roll, while sitting on the 'pot' the night before. Nobody needed to know that sacred synchronicity...and a golden wedding ring—a symbol of enduring love.

While home-schooling many years before...our curriculum was based on a concept of spiral learning—coming back again & again & again to the core objectives—revisiting and sometimes re-building on what, already learned...

That night—that first week of class—that priest, looked at me oddly—like I was some kind of 'odd-bird,' he couldn't fathom...

About 10 years later, I married that man...and the spiral learning...continues.

The Relic (a vignette)

A year ago, today—we planned a spiritual outing to commemorate my Jen's passing. We'd take a small bit of her ashes to Portland's sacred grotto—somewhere high above the city—she loved, so much.

It was a spur-of-the-moment gesture—Alan, always so eager to assist me in my quest for meaning. Lots to do quickly; feed the farm animals, shower, change. Almost ready to go, ok, quickly, I say to myself, get a small baggy, go get Jen's box of remains and fill it up—it'll be fine, you're all alone, I continue to say to myself. I bring it to the kitchen, carefully lift the lid, remove the silver marker and gently pull back the two plastic linings. Quick, quick, before anyone comes in, I think to myself again—so wanting to be alone with her. And then it, hits me. As my fingers slip into the container of what remains, that is physically her, I close my eyes. I am enraptured by the cool, sand-like substance. I feel spirit rise up from my belly. I'm like crazy-lady, again; I can feel her honey-blond hair in my hand; I can see her doleful big brown eyes and I dig deeper and deeper like I'm grasping at the sands of time—for gold. Amidst all the fine sand and small compressed balls of substance, I feel something of genuine form. Gently, I roll it over and over between my two fingers. Finally I open my eyes and look down at the grey ashen sand, to see; an infinitesimal, less than 3/4 of an inch long, perfectly formed, bone. It looks like a tiny finger or toe bone, possibly from a wrist or a hand or a finger—her finger! With my free hand, I cover my mouth as if to hold my spirit in or suppress my joyful squeal. I go running outside, looking for someone to share it with—Alan's just rounding the corner.

I carefully cup my hand at my chest and whisper, look—it's her. He acknowledges its exquisite beauty and exclaims, It's a relic! I smile and chuckle to myself about his religious choice of words. I smile back at him in wonder and say, Yes, but it's a tiny bit of her, intact.

(Fast forward—a year later...)

It's a year later—today—a ten year marker. I wake up to a dream of looking for golden slippers—real gold. I remember, that precious relic, where did I put it, for safekeeping??? (I lose many things this way.) I remember.

I set about arranging my little sacred tribute to Jen right behind my laptop. Perched on a stack of special books is a tiny portrait of her, framed by a pewter goddess pouring flowers from an earthen vessel, beside that, is me-- the paper mache' goldfish with rhinestone eyes, protective Quen Yin, looking over her, and a memento of hers—a tiny green plastic big-eyed alien with wry grin. (Just yesterday I read in her notes the question, Why are aliens evil? I can speculate what she meant by that; alien—other— a good lesson.) The last item is the small wooden box given me by my sister, containing the sacred Frankincense and Myrrh.

When my sister gave it to me for my birthday this year, I had wondered, I wonder where the gold will come from? Now, I get it—the gold would come from Jen as in my dream.

This morning, the golden slippers—pure gold, reminded me to look for the relic. In the dream, the golden slippers had exposed toes. Now I know that the bone is from her feet and I have placed it inside the wooden box—a snug fit, but just enough room for Frankincense, Gold and Myrrh—in that order.

How very fitting it is that as I symbolically punch through night today, many years ago the baby Jesus punched through the Night by being born in a manger and the Wise men brought Him gifts. Jen always loved the baby Jesus in the cradle and as a little girl with golden blond hair she lovingly hung that ornament on the tree every Christmas. Somehow, I feel that Jen and I and my sister Carole too, are bringing those very same gifts to the little baby Jesus, tonight—three wise women bringing gifts of love.

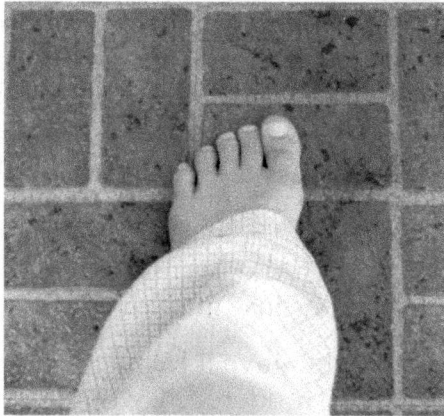

Golden Glow of Autumn

As the golden glow of autumn
turns to winter mush
I sit reposed by my cozy fire
grateful
that I have nothing--to do.

I look back at what life has
dealt me
and I am--at peace.

Harsh experience has taught me
that
it is at the broken places
that
sweet wine seeps out
if we let it.

It is at the tender places
 that
the spirit effervesces and
keeps us--soft to the touch.

Yes, experience can be
a harsh task-master, but
it's wisdom
is a sweet, deep, long kiss.

Beyond the Leaning Tree ...

Beyond the leaning tree, the mist thickens
and the trail shrinks to nothing.
do not despair, you're almost there
you're almost there — you're almost there.
Your legs & arms are weary and your
brain's like mush, but you're almost
there.

Your hopes have been dashed one
too many times, your heart shredded like
pulled pork — your eyes glazed over with
Life fatigue, but still you strain
to see.

Where the trail is gone and the cloud
en-vel-opes, you spot a faint small light.
It beckons — you follow and it leads you
to your heart's desire — not too far, but
yes — in the challenging space just
beyond the leaning tree.

Fingernail Moon ...

There you are ...

   the fingernail—in the clear dark night
sky

as crouching lion...

   You shot that lunar fragment & tossed
it afar

a reminder--a remnant of chawed-off finger-tips ...

   Something I gave you

a habit—we shared.

So ugly to see ...

   So sweet & lovely, the memory

Honolulu nights—you—crouching down—shooting
up ...

into that still dark night sky

commemorating... that delicate smallest of crescents.

There you are—faithful as the night—here—with me
...

Where Love Is ...

We don't always know...where love is.

Sometimes, we think that it's on the other side of the fence, where that green grass grows

or, up in the sky where winged-lovers fly free

or on the beach, where water washes away our footprints and the lines we draw

but...

love lingers long—long after we've gone—stitches, the tears—that don't seem to wanna mend

remembers—the good, the bad, and, the indifferent

oh—the indifference—is the worst

once heard a young black man say, that being ignored is the worst—love me—or hate me but, don't ignore me—treating me like I don't even exist

love is—where we are and where we 'choose' to 'see' one another—even in our differences—especially, in our differences

that's where love is...

A Single Bougainvillea Petal ...

One in a multitude—the only one seen—blushing pink, from exposure, fragile & thin-Skinned,

she reads.

* * *

Don't Know 'bout You, but

I know about me....

I'm still plumb-ing, the

>>> *Family tree....*

What Does a Poem Kill?

Killing my confusion, I write on and on and on—not knowing where I'm going—not caring about the outcome—I write. While we're at, let's kill FEAR—tearing at those empty threats and accusations—pulling at the threads—unraveling self-doubt and false humility. Faster and faster, I write, like the poem has a mind of its own and it does.

I ride it like a roller coaster bringing me back, time after time to face each of the enemies—picking them off, one-by-one, as I spot them, with my BB-gun of words.

Gradually, slowly we lose momentum as I'm running out of steam and confusion and dis-ease gives way to calm. Gone are the dreary obstacles to peace—killed off by the captain of my soul—the poem.

Nov. 30th 2011--ten years ago today--my daughter took her life--to heaven--ground zero for me.

Gentle Fall of Autumn Leaves

I missed the gentle fall of autumn leaves this season.

Now, I marvel at their rain-soaked perfect patterns beneath my feet.

Should I step on them, like a hapless, careless child-- or would that bad luck, bring?

Far too many to dodge--flames of color rising from the earth--red, gold, orange, brown.

Perhaps, I'll just breathe the moist fresh air that surrounds me and wait for autumn leaves to rise again.

What I Need ...

I need not strive so...

                        I need to let things unfold.

I've been pushing & propelling too much.

I am an Apple Tree...

I just grow & bear fruit.

I am a Gravenstein—not all like my apples.

Mine, are green, sharp & crisp.

They make really good apple pies, (smile)

to eat by the hearth

but not all are into that.

They will find me—

                    who are.

Patterns...

So much more important

             than they seem...

When I write poems — I shift

into auto-pilot...

I let the lines break where they will

and punctuation speak or

             Not...

I love a good paisley print

             In warm colors...

I'm not very ordered.

Yeah, patterns speak volumes —

I'm trying to listen.

T'was ...

T'was the worst of days

T'was the best of days...

Through the fragility of Circumstance

Life crept in...masquerading

As death...

Lifting the veil thin, it speaks

Of Love eternal & hopes deferred...

        For now—a

moment

96

Sunday …

It remains to be

seen

what cannot be

lived without...

Breath of Life, yet

dear and sweet

does not yet, extinguish

mortal flame.

What harbours deep

within

or renders deep

without

will take its toll in

own sweet time

of that,

I have no doubt.

The Ticking Clock

I'm not afraid
of the ticking clock.
Our days are numbered.
Our hairs are counted.

It's always a good day
to die.
It's never a good day
to die--
or something in between.

Woody Allen's been known
to say,
"I'm not afraid to die-- I just
don't wanna be there when it happens."

I'm not afraid to die.
I'm not afraid of
the ticking clock.
But then...

Lately, Alan's been ringing the
bell in the chapel, early
while I'm still asleep--
Sometimes, I hear it in my
twilight--I hear myself think--
involuntarily, "For whom the bell tolls,"
                    does it toll for me???

Sisters ...

In a yes-ter-year, far far away...we lived here.

We drank tea in the morning, ate home-made yeast-bread toast

slathered in real butter~ shared our fresh dreams and watched

the children frolic and grow.

We washed bedding, hung it in lines to dry in the golden sun-to be kissed by the California wind and to have those kisses returned to us when we lay down at night, to sleep.

Without cars, we all strolled to town—smelled the flowers along the way, giggled at everything and fingered the fine things the local merchants offered— we drooled-- bought our fresh food, dragged ourselves home, napped the children and prepared small feasts with wine & laughter & children's games...we lived here.

We waited for hubbies and tended our gardens, drank wine and listened to good music. Long, long ago— perhaps in other life-times—we lived here, in what seems—a simple life. It was never simple, but it was, pleasant...

Let's drink a toast to yes-ter-years & all the long, long ago ... sister.

Symbols ... From a Sandplay Workshop

I suppose it was the matruska that appealed to me the most, though I would call myself other things. I like the fact that it's made of wood that's shiny and smooth to the touch, pretty and that the colorful garb she wears is lovely. I like the surprise and delight of opening one and finding another and another and, yet another. I like that there is always something deeper to explore. I really do not feel that the little wooden figures are alive, so I don't know that they exhibit emotions. Perhaps it is that little yellow core creature inside—deep down, that writes the poetry and emotes that way.

It harkens back to some ancient family history that I glimpse as I look at, feel and explore the matruska. When I dress in my prim—Sunday go-to-meeting-clothes my priest friend says I look like something he calls a babuska—an orthodox priest's wife. That reminds me of my grandma from the Armenia/Russian border with her stout, square body and solid shoes and fringed scarf swathed about her head and shoulders. To me, "it", "they," "she" exudes a sort of primal heritage, a way of being, a connection of soul, to the earth...who knows...maybe, a sort of, home?

Love Shouldn't Hurt ...

Says the beat-up husband or
> *wife to the "other"*
Says the jilted lover
> *at the altar*
Says the unfulfilled — left with
domestic dreams of bliss
> *that will never be*
Says the parent standing
> *at a child's grave*
Says, being trapped in a body
> *that does not obey*
Love shouldn't hurt...
Says starving children, the
> *The world over,*
Through no fault of their own...

> *But sometimes, it does.*

As Someone's Papa Used to Always Say

As someone's Papa used to always say,

"There's something about that person that I don't like about me!"

Ok--let's do, "The Limbo Rock, How LOW, does that Limbo Pole go???"

The-- "Bother Me Threshold." The--"that bothers me, Limbo Pole..."

The--"I'm overly sensitive, vulnerable, fragile—React to everything Pole..."

"Stop That! Stop that right now Ms Claudia. You're better than that."

"Ok, let's NOT, do--The Limbo Rock."

Poetry Heals …

Thinking don't make it right…
Take you down a blind alley, it will
Where you'll be "punched out"
By alley cats & demon dogs
Left for dead — bloodied
In the ditches of your mind
Until the spell wears off
And your heart starts tickin'
In the blind spaces
And lickin' your wounds bone dry
Til' the sun starts shinin'
And healing words
Begin to stitch wounds too big
To pull together
In the just plain light of day.

Tarry with me & let's make beautiful music
with words spun together
by the silver and gold of hope, health and blind faith
of the heart
dancing down a river of dreams, reminiscent
of unobstructed veins and patched up leaks
leading to renewed vigor and purpose.
Yes-sir-ee — poetry heals…
                    Carry on, my friend.

San Francisco —

The luxury of being lost
In the masses
comraderie without effort
In the well-boundaried crowd
cheek-to-cheek on a cable car
hip-to-hip on a bus.
One wonders at the cosmopolitan lifestyle
where rain is not noticed
and time never sleeps.
The city sounds keeping the night watch
affording me snug haven
in my turn-of-the-century, hole-in-the-wall, hotel.
Neon lights, life affirming & threatening sirens
and people with a purpose going to and fro…
looking down on the sight daily
I am alternately energized & comforted
by this hearty crowd.
There is a little "city girl" in me, yet
a flame, fanned
in the city of my birth.

Let it Rain, Let it Rain, Let it Rain

Snug in my bed of billowy, cloud-like warmth
I purr to the gentle rhythm of raindrops on my roof.
Slowly, they build to a crushing crescendo—one note
at a time
each playing its drop in proper succession, pitch and
placement,
punctuated only by an occasional rooster crow and
the distant rumblings of God as He rearranges the
furniture
in His house—again & again & again it rumbles
until it's just right~
Perfectly arranged, is a cozy spot in the east window
to catch
the morning sun, should it decide to peek its head
above the trees,
tomorrow.
As tomorrow will come and take care of itself, it will--
but for now…
Let it rain, let it rain, let it rain
and wash away the night's debris
and play its soothing melody for me
'til dawn, when I'll say,

"Is the coffee ready?"

WATER ...

...replenishes the EARTH
drowns & destroys
quenches a thirst
cleanses, within & without
refracts the LIGHT
makes visible & enhances.

One can live longer without food than
WATER...
WATER—could be...
our most precious resource
at the very least, one of them
growing more scarce by the hour.
Without it, we perish.
With it, we flourish.
In it, we frolic—as exploring
an unknown universe.
Created on the second day—
God said,
"It is good,"
and it is.
WATER
Is good!

106

Am I Vintage, Yet?

Am I vintage, yet?
Am I full bodied & fine?
Have I been pressed & squeezed
plucked from the vine?
Nurtured in the counties
                of all things, wine?
Am I vintage yet? Am I vintage yet?
Is my oblong face
          in gray--
stored in dark places
              'til the end of day?
Have the decades of life
             had their way?
Am I vintage yet? Am I vintage yet?
Will I wake-up one day and
            find myself dead?
A season's yield—partakened
            with bread?
Poured from a wineskin
           leathered by sun
enjoyed by a dear heart
           not wont to run?
The wine of a more satisfying life
           sweetened by time
relaxes my mind
pressed from the lips of a more
           ancient rhyme—
It's true—it's true—perhaps, at long last—I am
           vintage wine.

Wired ...

Bird on a wire...

On winter's Dawn
        you'll find me here...
                As perched upon a wire
longing to unfold widespread
        wings, soaring freely above the fray
I find myself tied to this earth
        through interest, need or calling
                call it what you may.
So, here I sit perched
        from afar
                a tiny little nondescript wingling
        twittering on occasion
                or swooping in for closer look
                        or
        displaced with feet in tethered group
                more often than not
                        content
        to watch, to wait, to observe, to...
                assimilate
                to pray, to contemplate, to stay...

I'm a writer...on a wire.

Wind & Rain ...

She closed her window
and turned away
when wind and rain
came to town.

She pulled a book
off the shelf
and stuck her nose
in it...

She fluffed her pillow
and fell asleep.
She counted chickens
instead of sheep.

The garden--depleted
filled with chicken manure.

She became an ostrich
and fluffed her feathers
for warmth.

She dreamed of green
pastures beyond the hedge
but couldn't see them
from where she stood

tho' it's true-- she wasn't
                        looking.

Then, tornado hit—sending
house adrift on
windswept waves
foundation cracked and
sent asunder—
a crater, where once
home-sweet-home
had been…

The seasons passed again and again
 and again
with them, snow, sun, wind and
rain and more rain.

Now perched in sturdy tree
above the site—she trills
her lonesome freedom song
to wandering herds of sheep,
cows and other assorted
creatures of the hill…

as they drink deeply
from the crater that
mourning dove--filled
                        with her tears.

110

After They've Gone ...

Tiny handprints left on the on the
                                    window
to remember...
fairyland trails to everywhere
                        and
sticks, sticks, sticks
                        everyplace I look...
Who knew—an ordinary stick
                        a treasure was.
Pine cone mountains here & there
sandplay scenes frozen in
                        time
scores of candid shots set to
'You Gotta Friend in ME'—who
switched the song on the 'puter'???
Sweethearts—dear hearts—too
                        Wonderful for me...
set free in the forest...
                        my little fam-i-ly.
The swing set—never touched—nature
                        beckoned better.
Generations of lovin' here...
I (heart) U too, Isa!
Are you still smiling Jenny dear &
                        drinking champagne???
God Luv Ya!
                        Skol!

Healing is a Lifelong Lesson ...
and Then Some ...

She called me Claudja
After passing, she's told me many things...

Things I couldn't hear
Things I wouldn't hear
Things I needed to hear
Things I hoped to hear
all manner of things...she told me.

She warned of my daughter's death
five months prior.
I couldn't hear...
She told me of the ancient
truths
I wouldn't hear...

She told me, 'Ev'ry thing would
be alright'
I had to hear...
And to this very day I
hold that very dear!

'Little Grandma with the sun
glasses', we called her (from Armenia)
They weren't sunglasses but
we kids 'knew'--they had
protected her from the glaring
desert sun she marched thru' on
her journey here--to Amerika!

I love you Little Grandma, Claudja

Hardening of the Hearteries ...

Mid-August...the world goes even more crazy...chemical weapons...used...world politics ratchets up...my sister gets sick...I get sick...in response...

At many times...

It pains me to live in this world. I've had just enough happen to me and mine, to almost join the legions of those who question the very existence of a loving God...who careth...for us.

So many people doing so many good things—so many committing horrific crimes against humanity, by mistake, by omission, by intention. What will become of us??? The human race??? You & me???

I retreat in prayer, in pain, in purpose—as if it might go away, in time—I just can't stomach it! I feebly attempt to clean-up my little acre—only to find out, it's not as easy as it sounds...

Does anybody care???

I stay away from those I love—hoping I can spare them—my presence—could be contagious, I think— my gut instinct—my self-diagnosis—I suffer from Hardening of the Hearteries—put me away gently—I pray thee—sooner rather than later. I must harden my heart some, in order to survive, it seems. What will you do with that???

Celebrating Jennifer 1973-2001 ... the BEST Bad-Ass Girl a mama ever had ...

*No bullshit artist... calling things as they were
Creative to the core... colorful as fireworks*

*Spitfire girl... truth to power... Tupac to Tariq Dealt
a heartbreak hand... survived... for a while*

*Cool, wry sense of humor
Deep... as the abyss...*

*Proud to be your mom... and yes... I probably... at
times*

Reflect you... as... the moon... of a million face

*MISS YOU... like the sun in winter, here
Celebrating the life that you are...*

Happy Birthday Jen!!!

114

Someone Once Asked Me How I Can Read These and Not Cry

In response…

I have been with this sooo long—sooo hard—sooo deep

That…
It has become the 'nut' I live in…
Like an acorn nut.
I have a hard-shell finish
And yet…Some days, I think, it might just be my last—so deep is the pain…or not…depending, on the day.

It's not logical or right, I know
                              But

Please—bear with me
As long as I do no harm???
And—If, I do you harm—Please—Have mercy…
Put me away—gently—I'd do the same for you.

[Everything that has and comes to me is filtered through the fingers of Christ—it's allowed…therefore…"I can do or get through all things through Christ, who strengthens me."]

I must persevere…and I will…and I do…

Vanishing Words ...

WE really are a violent people in thought, word and sometimes, deed. Growing up, I always had this sinking feeling in the pit of my stomach whenever I'd see teachers grab a black felt eraser and whoosh away all the words on the board. Mesmerized I was, with a frantic sort of curiosity as they each in their own style snuffed out all the words, like pulling precious breath from a baby bird's beak.

Some swooched back and forth in big broad figure 8's with bold aggressive strokes. Others used choppy little back and forth movements haphazardly in every direction leaving me strangely irritated with the chaotic mess they left behind.

I found it all strangely annoying. I despised them without knowing why. Today—I think I get it it--vanishing words! For me, it was as if they were removing forever, the written word as censors throughout the ages had burned precious books at the stake and tyrannical families had "hushed" the innocent voice of victims of abuse, to protect "the family"—we'll call them. Church, state, household—it doesn't matter—it's all abuse in the family of man, woman and child—a crime against humanity. We could call them "The Wild Bunch," for they really are a violent people.

Words—freeing words, healing words, sacred words—forever silenced as when the teacher would make them vanish from the board, leaving nothing but the smeared remains of chalk dust wafting through the air, cutting off the breath from my nose—the bird's beak.

Fly away bird. Fly away swift and far and sing your anthem in the heavens where your words trail on forever—uncensored …

"Erase, erase, erase," I remember a young comic miming those same movements above his head… Speculating, I am how nice it would be if we could do that with our violent words—but we can't…erase, erase, erase. But we can, make space to let…the healing words begin …

The 'Little Movies'

that on occasion, riffle
through my mind
random memories when
all were still alive and we
gathered at holidays in chaotic
stress and boisterous joy
never knowing that, time does
not stand still and these moments
would not always be...

Or deeper still, from days
way back when three
sisters were like comrades
hunkered down in trenches of
war, fought on the home front...

Yes, remembering, the 'big dream'
dreamt a few years back of
a sacred alter inside a windswept
tent, amidst huge sandy hills
in an ancient Far East desert.
I was handed a precious family
film, cleverly and carefully hidden
in a fresh-baked round loaf of
bread — to be placed for safe-
keeping, under the alter and
shocked, and curious, I was, by the title...

"The Wild Bunch."

118

The Veil is Thin …

I take my meds, I attend all the meetings, I follow all the rules and still I hear the voice of God, was the impassioned outburst from the lad at the far end of the table. It was the first time I'd heard him speak in my several weeks of training at the forensic unit of the local in-treatment state-run mental unit. Silence fell over the room. I glanced quickly at my superiors who clearly didn't know how to respond. So, I thought to myself, psycho-spirituality was not addressed at the table—back to sterile discussions of insight, strategies and symptom control.

The young man with the soul-full eyes and the blue-black curls resembled a Raphael painting. He was beautiful! I wondered what he was there for. Everyone there was there for life, having done something unspeakable. He was so young. I wanted to cry. Clearly aware that my emotions were not appropriate to my clinical role, I retreated inwardly—the lesser of two evils.

It was while walking to that meeting that I first glimpsed the young woman I will never forget. She looked to be in her mid-twenties and was about five feet tall. She wore a loose fitting shirt, with baggy pants and an over-sized pink and white baseball cap that covered the top third of her head and face.

She walked close by me—unusual because we are cautioned to keep distance all about ourselves whenever on campus. Why did they call them east, west and middle campuses, I questioned myself. Were we supposed to learn something here? Instinctively, I averted my eyes from her as I witnessed

her disfigurement. Her eyes drilled into me. I tried to erase her image from my mind but I couldn't. Her face was deeply scarred from fire or chemicals, I suspected. Her mouth appeared painted on by a child's hand and her eyes were like two dark buttons recessed into skin stretched too tight inside two circles the size of two dimes. I don't recall a nose. I wondered, why physical disfigurement would land her in a place like this--perhaps, because she couldn't live out there in the world? This mental hospital was disquieting in so many ways!

I was on the fast track, trying to learn all I could to know how to help my daughter who had been in and out of psychosis and had tried different therapies and many powerful drug concoctions to no avail.

Thanksgiving was fast approaching. My school schedule was busy. Jen was not returning my calls and we were gathering at our place for the holiday. I was already feeling un-easiness in my being and then I saw this gal, again.

My friend and I were sitting at a table at McDonald's, about a block from the hospital. She walked right by us, again piercing me with her eyes. I stopped my friend mid-sentence and said, Beverly, did you see her? She looked all around and said, No, who? I answered her somewhat frantically, that scarred girl with the baseball cap? My friend looked at me with mild concern.

I rushed from there to the deli-counter of the nearby grocer for last minute Thanksgiving items. To my horror, at this point there she is again with the few people waiting their turn. Three times in less than three days—now I know that something significant is taking place. I just don't know what it is.

She appears to recognize me! The air feels heavy because everyone is avoiding her. I take a deep breath, swallow my fear and make eye contact with her. Her deep piercing eyes soften. My order is ready. I feel myself relax into her eyes and smile at her and wish her a Happy Thanksgiving. The veil separating spirit and flesh feels somehow thin.

We have Thanksgiving with everyone but Jen because she doesn't come—the absent elephant not in the room. Six days later, on her father's birthday—she's gone.

I'm convinced that the tiny little disfigured gal at Western State was somehow connected with Jen and me. My Jen, disfigured on the inside and unable to survive in this world, as she was and wanting to connect with her mom, one last time. Magical thinking perhaps or perhaps the mystery of human connection in a careless world.

Sacred Place/Sacred Space

Remembering a young mother of three in Holy Spirit boot camp frantically running to that prayer closet in the master bedroomwith makeshift alter, all the way in—no matter, what was on it
it was my place of refuge
when the demons would daily scream at me that I wasn't worthyand I couldn't be close to the Lord because of something horrible, in my own eyes that I had just done.

I'd run to my alter, fall on my knees and sing,
"The Name of the Lord is a strong and mighty tower
The Name of the Lord, is a refuge for my soul.
The Name of the Lord is a bulwark I can lean on…"

That's where I'd run.
It worked for a while—though I felt a little obsessive
And it did get cumbersome.
(It was our secret—we had a lot of them—Holy Spirit & I)

The next phase was to stop running to the prayer closet so often
And so frantically.
Oftentimes, I was caring for the children—cooking, cleaning, playing in the backyard, going for walks.

I was advised to sing those songs of refuge & praise quietly while doing my everyday activities much as the Negroes of old, sang their spirituals in the fields of the South. I even had a friend—Catherine, a big black mama visiting from the slums of Washington D.C. to show me how to do it. She didn't know she was teaching me, but she was. I made her and her family meals, she insisted on washing the dishes and singing. She said that God told her to come to Tulsa and learn from me how to teach the children. She was teaching me how to survive my life.

I was learning spiritual life in the trenches, one day at a time.

*   *   *

These days—some thirty years and many happy and sad dramas later, I'm glad I spent those days in boot camp. It was there that I eventually learned to move that prayer closet to the inside of me and live there every moment of the day— 24/7. It didn't matter if I was scuba diving some thirty feet under the sea or photographing sky-divers from a helicopter ten thousand feet above or anywhere in between, God was with me and that is and was my sacred place.

I don't inhabit churches as I did back then for reasons unfathomable and unimportant but I do still worship the same God and I find that God everywhere—in the faces of my friends and my enemies, in the hopes and dreams of people everywhere, but I prefer to find it in nature and solitude, preferably far from man's debris. Call me a coward, call me a hermit or better yet, call me by my name. My outings are few and far between and that is the way I like it. I have enough memories to warm my heart for a long long time and while my arms are open wide, I embrace my own heart as well and try to give it what it needs. It is after-all, to me, a very sacred space.

Nothin' New Under the Sun ...

Pining for a creative
thought, I am.
Nothing.
All my thoughts come from
somewhere,
inside, outside and around...
Those who were there
when my life shattered
when my earth shook to the core?
They know who they are--mortal angels
sent on shafts of Light
some with ears, some with shoulders
some with arms, some with words
some with silence and a bottle of wine
or a chalice.

But I would be a liar and a cheat
if I did not fess-up
when asked
who was my steady side-kick
who was with me--always
even when I did not know
Emmanuel--God with me!

Never Thought I'd Live to See

...

me live "so" many lives...
Never thought I'd live to see...
"Black Friday," eclipse both
Christmas & Thanksgiving...
watch out Halloween!
Never thought a heart could
break & mend, again & again
and again...
Frankenstein stitches on my heart
or velveteen pillow with cross-stitch
embroidery with tiny daisies & whip
stitch & such...

It's good. It's good. It's "all" good as
Tyler would say. Have a good day--
happy face--with a bullet hole in the
forehead--feeling sardonically silly. ;) NOT!

Happy Black Friday!

Hermitage Cedar

O graceful drooping

hermitage cedar

planted upon arriving

six long years ago

aggressively mispruned

by Whither-goat's every escape

sweet memories forever...

*   enthroned*

not the fantasy of perfection

I longed to see

but memories instead

of Life's frailty

today your crown reaches

above the spire

our very own sacred cedar...

*   Deodar.*

Bring on the Animals ... Jimmy Dean

Bring on the animals...

Me and horses never got along
as far back as I can
                    remember...
at seven, my Brownie group
went horse-back riding
in the Sonoma hills...
I no sooner got on and that
Huge 'being' ran off with me
through hills and dales and
dried out river beds.
I could hear the far off cries...
' hold on and put your head down'...
not soon enough to keep
my face from being slashed
by the dried-out summer oaks
                    I so loved...
must've blacked out—don't even
remember with my mind the
rest of that story
but the body remembers.
Next—I'm fifteen—my new
boyfriend and his best friend
want to go riding in the Santa
Cruz hills with his 'horsey-girl
friend'—too shy to let on my
fear... I ride, only to be bounced
around so hard—I excuse myself

to the restroom to find the trauma
so severe I start my period
right then and there two weeks
early—never done that before… or since.
Now, thirty years old, on a ride
near Wenatchee with husband and
three children—trying so hard
to be brave for the kids…
right along the river's edge…
no mishaps—just internal
drama and trauma.

2001—fifty-one years old
daughter takes her own life
thirty-four year marriage is
                              over.

The earth opens up and
swallows me…
A friend loans me his
twenty-six foot trailer…
another friend hooks me
up in her tree-lined backyard
right next to the barn and
                  horse corral…

She wants me to rest and
grieve in a safe close place (thank God for friends!)

My little windowed spot, with
computer and myself, is right next
to the fence…
Nightly, I awake, sit in my dark spot and

sob and cry and sometimes, just sit
in the dark and 'feel' the nothingness

the void.
One night, I hear the un-familiar sound
of an almost inaudible snort and what sounds
like—a gentle blowing of air through closed lips???
I peer into the darkness outside my window
to see a big horse-head just inches from
my face.

He's nudging close as he can get
Beckoning me...
His sounds and heart embrace
like a healing salve...
                    I cry...

tears of gratitude and yes—even joy.
It's nice to be heard and seen.
We become regular late-night
companions...

my intuitive healing friend
                    'Jimmy Dean' and I.

It Behooves Me to Not

believe in a literal hell
with unending fire and torment
that waters can't quell.

I have opened Pandora's fictional
box of unwanted thoughts
little by little
breaking the locks...

of generations of gloom
resulting in harm
sprinkled, with laughter and tears.

Laugh, so you won't cry.
Paint rainbows on you lids
and play, the clown.
And why do you do this?
Wisely, you might ask...

Because, life goes on, my dear
life goes on, for some, as I've
Heard it said...
long—after, the thrill is gone.

Moved to the country—to
Forget it all
Only—to re-member...
all the broken pieces.
Funny—how that works.

The Kiss of Grace...

I have experienced the
Awe-ful Grace of God
on the cheeky side of
Midnight.
I have wallowed in my own
Mire.
I have felt the companionship of
Sorrow.
I have felt the kiss of 'nothingness,'
 The 'Void'...
Until...
I suffered—to avail
until...
I drank the bloody wine of
Redemption
until...
I fell, in blissful surrender to
Night's Joy!

> *I am broken. I am broken. I am unbelievably*
> *brokenly*
>> *Whole.*

The Older I Get ...

The older I get…
The less I think I know.
Alas, the pressure's off
A release of control, perhaps?

Holidays loom — the world
so big & busy & fragile.
I'm want, to travel — easier
in my sleep — unencumbered
by me.

Reunions take on an amber glow
time & space, revealed.
What's real — what's not
becomes a minor point.

I think therefore I am — not!
I feel because I can???
I care, because it's my
last vestige — of hope.

The world goes on, fashioned
for the tiniest visitor.
I'm smaller than I was
bigger than I hoped
re-united, with all…that matters.

Pay it Forward ... Pass it On

...

When push comes to shove
whatayagonnado??? Turn the other
cheek—or give back what ya think's due?
Much of what goes on is hidden
 like that behind the veil...of
what really is.
I think of whom I hold most dear and
what is good for them...
We're not any of us...long for
for this world—we'll be remembered
by the memories we've made.
Opportunities pass us by
like sand through our fingers.
Maybe that's part of why writers write and
artists paint—it's sharing our wares
our hopes and our dreams.
I'm thinkin' at any cost, must
keep up the good 'fight'—maybe, it means
keep on writin'—for what it's worth, so I can
pay it forward...pass it on...
and keep on...keepin' on...

Food for the children of the

      Non-GMO kind.

133

November Rising ...

November's rising and I feel
pilgrimage coming on.
I've got my eyes fixed on the prize.
Don't know how I'll get there.
Don't know when I'll do it,
　　　　but I will.

I'll ride the North Star
to that northern shore.
I'll watch her ashes dance
like dragonfly wings
on fresh-permed ocean waves.
I can already feel her spirit cold on my face—
the off-shore breeze powerful—deafening—
exhilarating!

I'll walk the sands of that familiar place, alone but not
alone.
I'll revisit places we made sacred with our silence and
our tears.
I'm already there.
I can taste the home-fries and the fresh-cooked eggs
Sunny-side up!
I can see my sweet-faced slippered friends—
at home among strangers—kindred spirits.
Yeah—I feel it!
November's rising in my veins—
Calling me...

Not to Jerusalem, or Mecca or Compestela

de Santiago or to Rome
        but
to Mokeleia—North Shore, Oahu
just beyond Wialua-town
Wanna come? Nah, I didn't think so. Don't wait up
for me.

I just might not return...

So Many Last Times ...

Oh my dilley, dilleys...
lavender, rose, trillium and lilies
and assorted birds of paradise...
to name, a few...
Our meetings have been so sweet
these thirty days past—I have wandered
in your garden deep and tasted
many a soulful treat.

On this, my day of days...
I am buoyed by the experience of
closeness, shared
tho' I realize this particular year
I have not engaged so.
Please know, never has it meant
that I was not there—I was.
I have plucked the sweetest of
bouquets and placed it on the the altar
of my remembrance—on this my
D-Day—my day of days
I remember, my baby girl...

Auf wiedersehen meine liebschens...
until—another November day...

Thank you for being there...with love, Claudia

136

Alas ... "Work" on My Epitaph—"She Did Her Work!"

I get through
another nasty November
still charged with memories
of personal tragedy & loss
as thin layers of eye-watering
onions, again peel
I did my 'work,' in
cozy, safe, community
layer-by-layer, I
muddled through
to—today
the ultimate end.

Thank you—my laughing, crying
Bleeding, writing friends.
We, did it together
endured to the end...
of yet, another November.

Godspeed my sweet jenny dear
                    stand tall and journey on...
                              mom loves
you...

Prepared ...

I am prepared for nothing
I am prepared for everything
I close my eyes...and wait. ~C

Empty Slippers...

The tide came in that day and washed your ashes far away. Never was a sound heard, a sight seen— just slipped you 'neath the surface of a dream.

Exhilleratin' was the culmination of kindred flare—not a soul 'round to stare.

How many days 'til you reached horizon's line— succumbed to the setting sun—ready to form in wiser, fresher, flesh, rising on the beams of dawn's new day.

I run to capture those, "empty slippers"—still have 'em, I do.

They remind me of you and every day we had... and memories... too numerous and wonderful to count....

Good day... Good night... Good morning.

Ghosts ...

Gone are the ghosts of Novembers' past

The writing, the crying, the walking, the

'time'

that they say heals, is working.

I know the ghosts of somewheres' past

Are sitting 'round a campfire bright

But hanging with those who keep love's

Memories alive

Incorporating her into our very own beings

Have

Teased out the brighter side of darkness.

I see her twinkle in my grandkids' eyes

Hear her laugh in their childlike glee

Snuggle with her in sleepy-time naps

'stuffies' clutched close to their hearts.

Life 'does' go on, even if not the way we

Planned

140

The ghosts of Jenny, Jen & Jennifer

Have taken on another skin

The skin I see, the whole world over...

We 'will' begin, again.

claudia, mom & mamacita

Another Kiss of Grace...

It was a relationship forged in the fire—he—rough times at work and the end of a 7 year Doctoral thesis and book project—me—the end of a 34 year marriage, menopause and worse yet, the loss by suicide of my only daughter. We didn't stand a chance in hell—or so it seemed.

We muddled through the courtship and shared the dream, of a peaceful parcel of land in the country—he—for a Hermitage—me—for a place to call 'home'—where my kids and grandkids could enjoy & a place for 'me' to 'retreat.'

At long last, we found the 'perfect' 10 acre 'place' with 'falling down cabin.' I, haltingly, moved up, in trailer. My dear friends sent me off with the only 'Rhodie,' I ever loved. I had long admired their small Rhodie tree with its annual flush of perfect white clusters, early on, tinged with pink. Upon leaving her backyard sanctuary, with trailer in tow, she handed me their gift—a five gallon Rhodie of the exact same variety as hers.

She handed it to me with love, concern, and pride in her eyes and said, "Here, this will bloom when you two are ready to wed." She 'knew' our rocky start.

I planted it lovingly outside the picture window where the curved tree grows and tended it faithfully, while he labored in love, on that falling down 'shack.' He had the vision of 'home.' I had the vision of the 'Rhodie' and 'family.' I loved the plant—I tended the plant and watched it grow, in its own unusual leggy, creative, un-Rhodie-like style. I loved it—but— no bloom.

Years passed—still, no bloom. I put it out of my mind. Then—one May—it bloomed—2 perfect fluffy blooms! We took pictures and made our engagement announcements from its lovely sensual interior.

We married, garden-party style, to a gathering of sixty. We tended the land, the critters, and continued our rocky struggle to meld our personalities and flourish—egos collided with flesh but we persevered …

Then, 6 years from that one blooming—following, his finishing—finally—really, finishing, that big fat book and me, publishing my very first book of poems—a tribute to the journey of the pain and hope of having lost my child—it bloomed again—leggy branches going every-which-way, in a chaotically ordered style, very similar to our melding process. Not one or two, but five blossoms of exquisite beauty, bloomed outside our picture window–FIVE–the number of Grace–Five–the number of people in my original family of procreation.

It warms my heart. It thrills my eye and to us, it is a sign in nature of the beautiful fruit tasted, of a long, hard, rocky road, finally realized. Grace has saved the days … and we are grateful, hopeful, and delighted. We look at it every day and marvel at the second kiss of grace. And yes, I realize, that it was grace all along that brought us this far and grace that will take us, all-the-way, down-the-road.

This is It ...

the nadir of my calendar year.
I feel myself--crouching lion
phoenix rising--from the bottom
of the sea
gathering strength in my hind
legs--to thrust myself upwards
through, to the surface--
punching a hole in the
night.

Ahhh yes...eye-piercing
Light and life-giving air
support me with a
new start...
reward, for patiently waiting
hidden,
within, the womb of time.

I think I'll call it-- November Rising.

147

Two Thoughts in Closing ...

Many years ago I had a dream while enrolled in a Social Service/Mental Health class (Abuse in the Family) at Pierce College in Washington State ... before my daughter's death ...

I saw a candelabra that resembled a Menorah, only the candles, I believe, 7 of them, were arranged in a circle, like a Ferris wheel. The candles were all perfect and unused, and none, of them had been lit. I heard the term, "mourning wheel." As I thought about the dream, I thought of many things. I thought about the Stations of the Cross and the sacraments. I thought of myself as a potential helper. I thought of all my losses that I had never grieved. I thought of abuse in the family. I wondered, if perhaps, each candle might stand for a station, of sorts, and provide an opportunity for working through the grief, the loss of 'whatever.' And I thought, until it's worked through, you really have nothing to give, except an 'ear' and that's something, but no compassionate insight, no deep understanding, no profound healing power. I thought, we have to be willing to go there—to each station, to each wound, to each loss and light the candles, pray the prayers—do what we must do and be healed. And guard yourself from people who would call it, a "whining wheel." I don't know about you, but I know "helpers" who haven't done that work yet and it shows. I'm 'working' on it.

148

And Finally …

And finally … while going through Jen's special box this last time, I came across a literary art publication from the University of Washington, Tacoma, where Jen and I had both been students and I had submitted her photo in memory of her. They chose it for their cover in 2003. A copy of the note I had sent with it, forgotten by me and folded and hidden inside its pages, brought back very real memories. This is it …

This is Jen. She was a precious and authentic human being. She was a university student like you and me—well, not quite–she was diagnosed three times with bipolar disorder and three times with schizoaffective disorder, depressive type with PTSD from a traumatic event (goes to show 'labels' are not set in stone). She experienced severe and distressing episodes the likes of which, you and I can only begin to imagine.

Don't pity her. Don't patronize her. Try to understand her. Believe her when she says that she sees cats out of the sides of her eyes. Listen to her and be of some assistance to her and the likes of her. Most importantly, cherish her while she's with you, because you will miss her when she's gone. I know I do …

Jen's Mom

Jennifer Patchen (1973-2001)

About the Author

Claudia Patchen has written her entire life, but is just now coming out of the closet of her dreams as a poet and author–with a little help from her friends. She has now published poetry, prose, and has been recognized for her photography and community service throughout the world.

Claudia has a master's degree in pastoral counseling and has been extensively trained as a sandplay therapist, but now she spends most of her days at a ten acre "Hermitage" on the Key Peninsula in Washington state, that she and her husband have labored in love to create. They abide there with assorted beloved critters.

www.ingramcontent.com/pod-product-compliance
Lightning Source LLC
Chambersburg PA
CBHW060253050426
42448CB00009B/1627